Handbook
Of
CHORD SUBSTITUTIONS

By Andy LaVerne

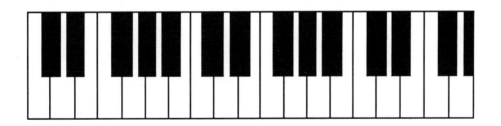

© 1991 Ekay Music, Inc.
333 Adams St., Bedford Hills, NY 10507

Table Of Contents

Text

Music

How To Create Your Own Substitute Chords And Reharmonizations

1

Two phrases come to mind when I look at the title above: "If it ain't broke, don't fix it," and, "better than new." Before you begin to manipulate a tune harmonically, you must first determine what the musical motivation is behind the change. Generally, I find that the tunes which come under consideration most often for harmonic alteration are of the "Tin Pan Alley" era. They have been around for quite a while, and have been interpreted by many fine artists.

Saying that these tunes are familiar is understating the fact. Some might argue that we should remain true to the composers' original intent, and therefore should leave all the harmonies intact ("If it ain't broke . . ."), while others feel that this material could benefit from a fresh approach ("Better than new"). Being a composer, I can empathize with the former statement. Yet, as a composer I feel that it is essential to give the performer creative license to interpret material in a personal manner.

The purpose of this book is to demonstrate techniques used to create substitute chords and reharmonizations. A collection of tunes will be presented, each receiving two special harmonic treatments. The first special treatment employs a mild use of substitutions, using the original harmonies as a guide. The second treatment will be a more advanced reharmonization, making use almost exclusively of alternative harmonies. Each tune is voiced out for two hands in a solo piano format. These voicings can be analyzed and transferred to your piano "vocabulary" for use as you see fit. Along with this selection of familiar standard tunes, I have included my own original blues. These suggest some alternative blues progressions, and they can be precursors for composing your own material. The process of finding chord substitutions is actually the first step in this direction.

This book can be used in several ways. Read the text and refer to the cited music examples; create your own versions of tunes using the techniques described; play through the music and see if you can extract some ideas to apply to other tunes. Play through the music and make note of other chordal possibilities for the given examples. You can also use the musical examples as a source for chord voicings.

Creative license is the key to creating your own substitute chords and reharmonizations. However, creativity should not be the only criterion for developing sub chords and re-harms. There are certain theoretical procedures which can be employed to aid in the search for alternative harmonies. Along with the pure creative process and music theory, the third part of this equation is to let your ear guide you. When I'm working on a tune, looking for a fresh harmonic setting, I draw upon all three to aid in the process.

Let's take a look at some techniques which can be used in the search for substitute chords.

Tritone Substitution

2

One of the most frequently called upon substitutions in the professional musician's bag of tricks is known as the *tritone substitution*. Generally speaking, this describes the fact that a dominant 7th chord can be replaced with another dominant 7th whose root is a tritone away from the original. A tritone is the term used to describe an interval (the distance between two notes) of three whole tones. This interval can also be referred to as an augmented fourth or a diminished fifth.

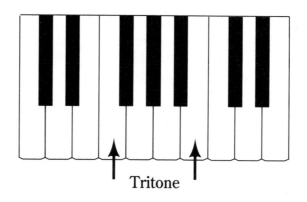

Tritone

For example, a G7 can be replaced with a Db7.

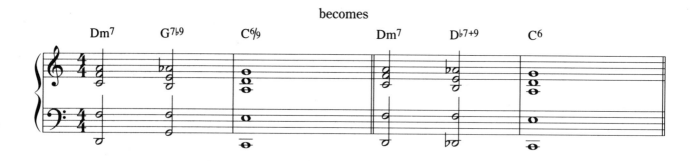

These chords are closely related in that they share two very important tones, F and B.

Here are further examples of tritone substitution.

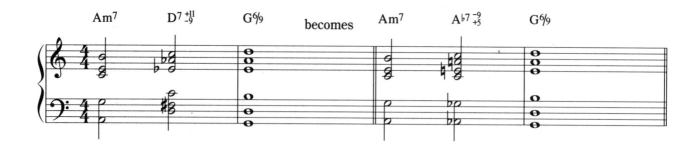

6

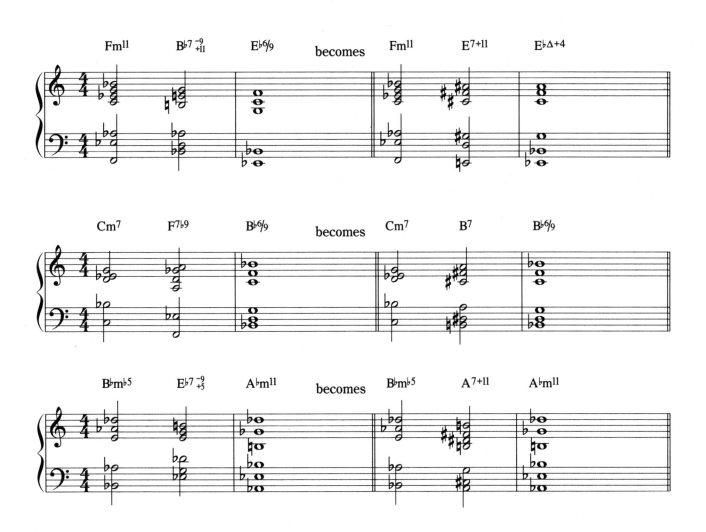

After playing through the examples above, you'll want to try your hand at creating your own. Here's a progression that moves from F to B♭ to E♭. How would you alter it using tritone substitution? I've indicated how I did

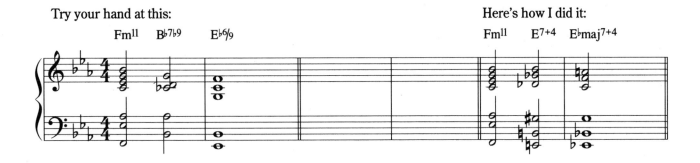

Now study this example of tritone substitution in "Darn That Dream," then, look at the other arrangements in this book to search for additional places in which this device is used.

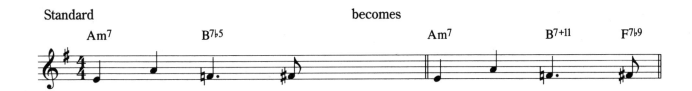

Changing Chord Qualities

3

The quality of a chord (major, minor, dominant, diminished, etc.) can be changed to another quality, even when you are keeping the same root. This can dramatically alter the mood of a piece or phrase. For instance, we can take a major quality chord and change it so that C becomes Cm or Eø Maj.7 becomes a diminished chord with a major seventh.

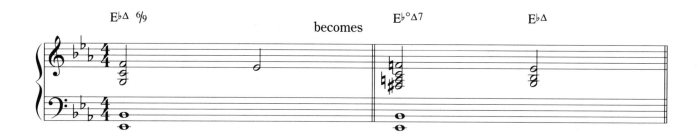

We can use the same principle for interchanging chords of other qualities. For example, we can take a minor chord and change its quality to major, dominant, half-diminished, or diminished.

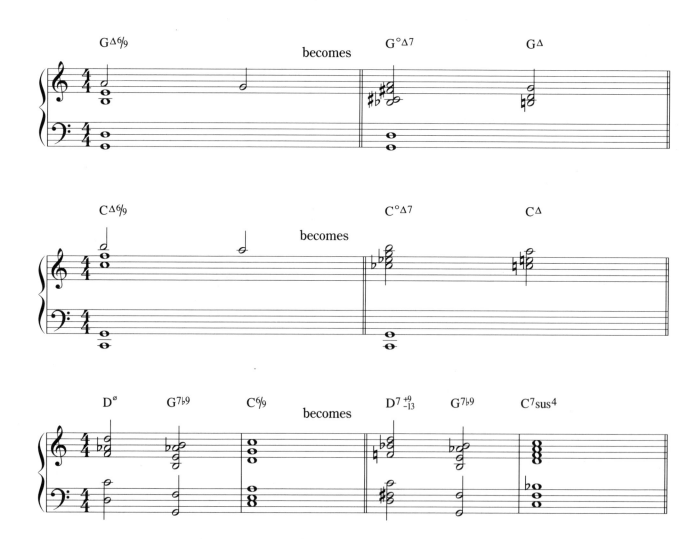

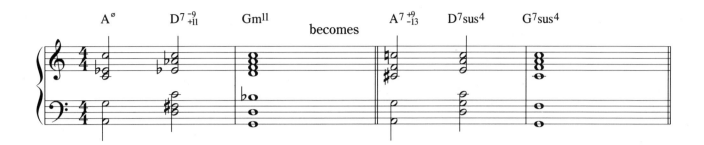

Try changing the following progression. I've indicated one possibility.

Try your hand at this:

Here's how I did it:

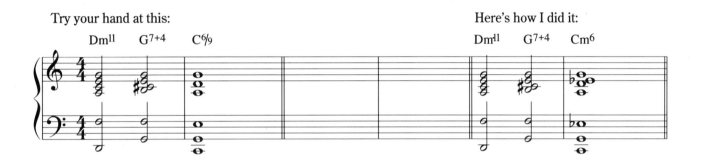

I used this device in my arrangement of "Cherokee."

Using Functional Harmony

4

Additional chords may be inserted into the harmonic rhythm of a song by following traditional patterns of chord resolution. For example, think of the fact that a dominant chord resolves easily to its tonic. If we have an E♭ chord we can almost always precede it with its dominant (B♭7). Other possibilities include inserting the ii chord before a V chord. Therefore if we have a G7, we can precede it with a Dm7.

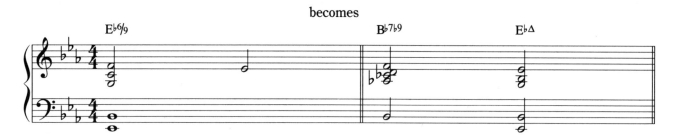

This can be carried a step further by inserting the ii chord's dominant (A7) before that ii chord. Yet another ii chord can be inserted in front of this chord, producing the progression Em7, A7, Dm7, G7. Any of these ii chords can be switched to a dominant quality, i.e. E7, A7, D7, G7. A IV chord is sometimes used in place of a ii chord, i.e., F, G7 instead of Dm, G7. Diminished chords can be used to good effect as well because of their strong tendency toward resolution: B°, C.

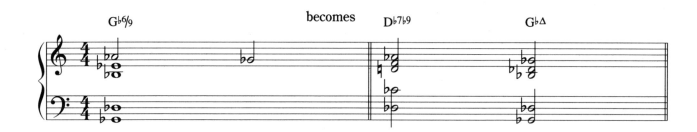

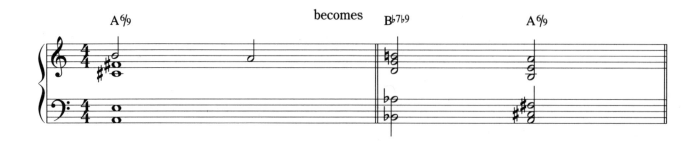

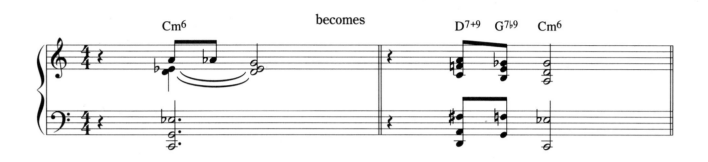

Try your hand at this: Here's how I did it:

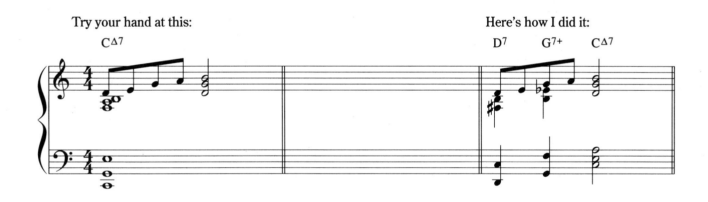

Here is how I used this device in "My Melancholy Baby."

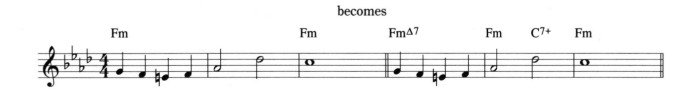

Using Non-Functional Harmony

5

Chord progressions can be used in which the traditional tendency of chord resolution is not apparent. This type of chordal movement involves *arbitrary* root movement. Experimenting with root movements of varying intervals can help in this process. Since there are no set theoretical rules to follow in this instance, final decision on the acceptance of a particular progression should be based on your ear and musical taste.

Here are some examples of the use of non-functional harmony.

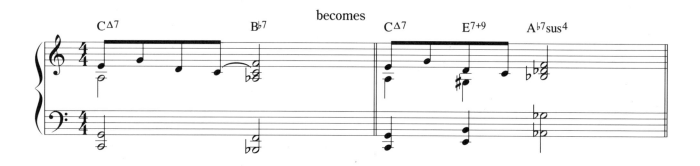

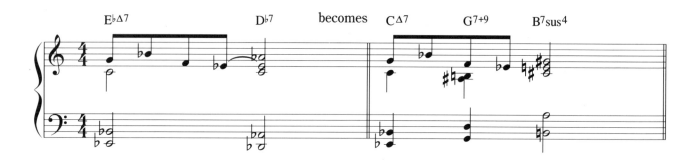

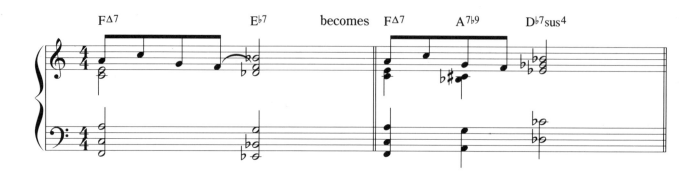

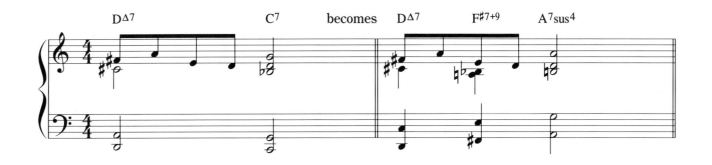

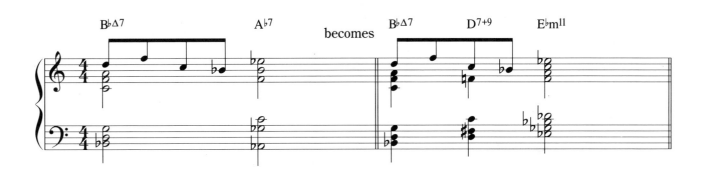

Try your hand at this: Here's how I did it:

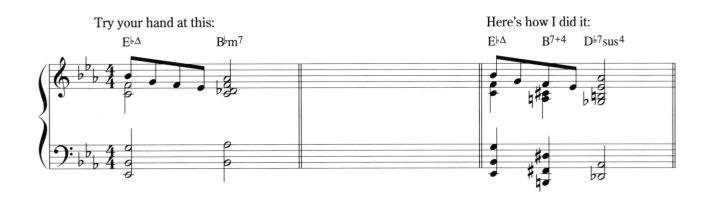

I used this device in "My Melancholy Baby."

becomes

Alterations Of Chord Tones

6

The color and mood of a chord can be changed or enhanced by adding *color tones* (chord extensions), and by altering the actual members of the chord (raising or lowering them in half step increments). The chord extensions (also known as color tones or upper structure triads) can be found by building an additional chord in thirds above the basic one we find in the music. If we take a G7, starting from the root, we have: G (root), B (3rd), D (5th), F (7th), to which we can add A (9th), C (11th), E (13th). Any of the tones can be raised or lowered by half steps to yield alterations to the color or quality of the chord. Using this technique can give a progression a very rich and colorful sound.

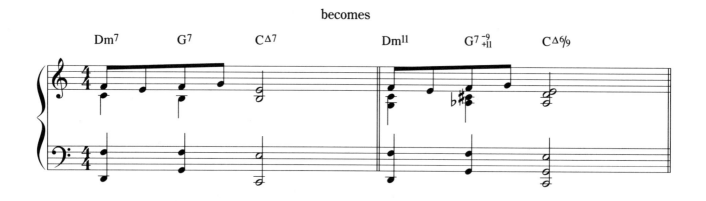

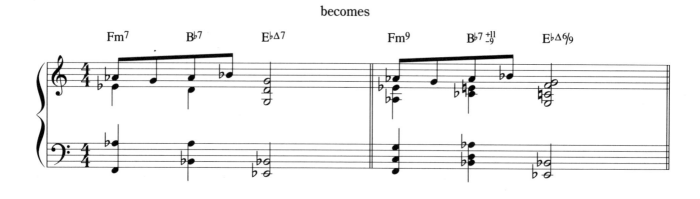

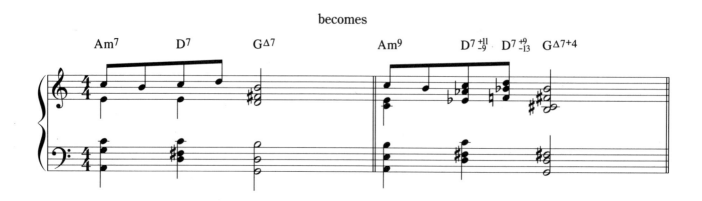

becomes

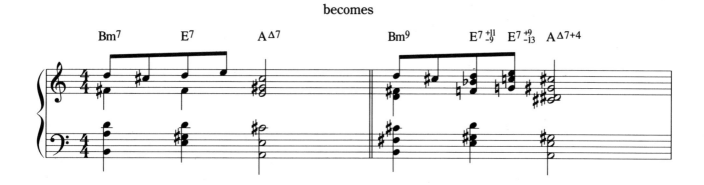

becomes

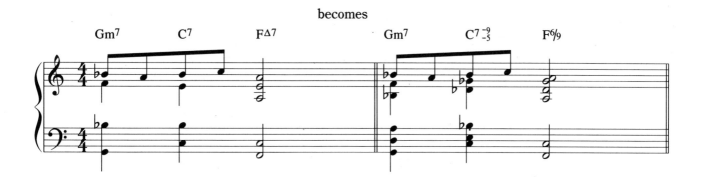

Try your hand at this: Here's how I did it:

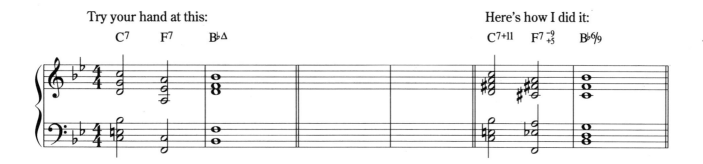

Here is how I used this device in "Wrap Your Troubles In Dreams."

becomes

Approaching Chords From Above Or Below

7

If a chord is established as a harmonic goal, it can always be approached by another chord. The half-step above approach is probably the most commonly used (D♭7 to C). The typical V7, I of G7 to C now becomes D♭7, C, which can also be viewed as the tritone substitution of D♭7 for G7. We can also leave the G7, C intact and approach the G7 with a dominant seventh chord from a whole step above: A♭7, G7, C.

There are many variations possible using the *approach* technique. Chords can also be approached from a half-step below the target chord (B7, C), from a whole-step above (D7, C) from a whole-step below (B♭7, C), or by a combination of these (D7, D♭7, C). Chord qualities can also be interchanged (minor instead of dominant, half diminished instead of minor). A series of back relating dominant chords can be used to approach a target chord. The term back relating dominant refers to a series of dominant chords each preceded by its own dominant (E♭7, A♭7, D♭7, C).

becomes

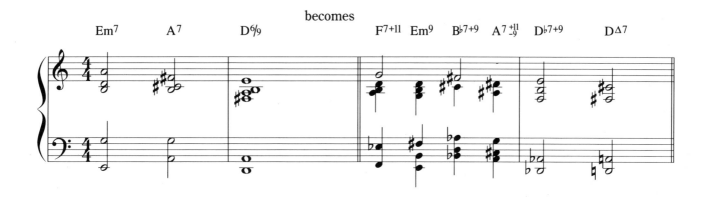

becomes

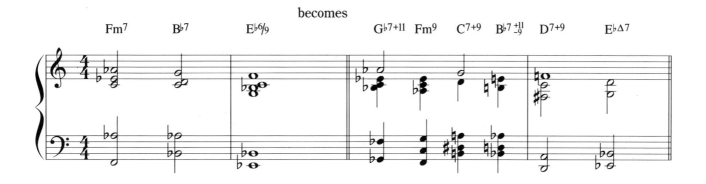

Try your hand at this: Here's how I did it:

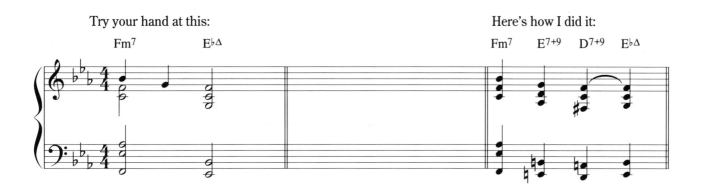

I used this technique in the following way for my arrangement of "Wrap Your Troubles In Dreams."

becomes

Functional Substitutions

8

Chords which share several common tones can be used interchangeably. This works well when chords share similar tendencies toward resolution. A functional progression such as C°7, F7(♭9) can substitute for A°7. The common tones found in these chords (C, E♭, F♯, A) as well as the resolution of both sets of chords to B♭ make this a viable substitution. Conversely, F♯°7 can replace the progression of A°7, D7(♭9). Along with the common tones (F♯, A, C, E♭) and resolution tendencies shared by these chords, they are also on the same *diminished axis*. A diminished axis is the series of tones formed by stacking minor thirds (the interval structure of the diminished seventh chord). Other commonly used substitutions are: the iii chord in place of a 1 chord (common tones), and the V°7 in place of a I chord (common tones).

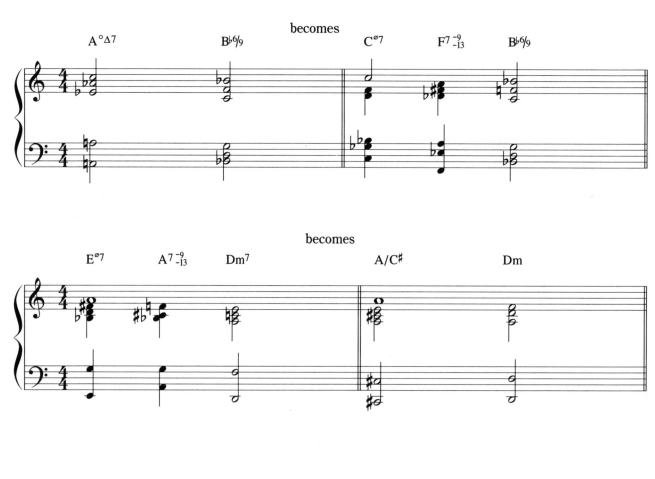

18

becomes

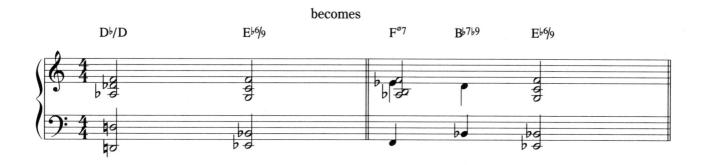

becomes

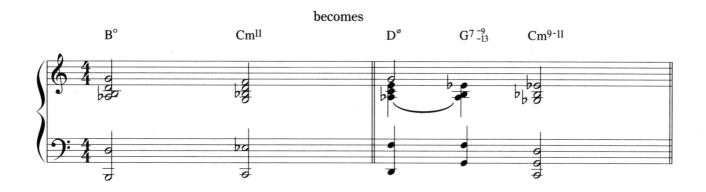

Try your hand at this: Here's how I did it:

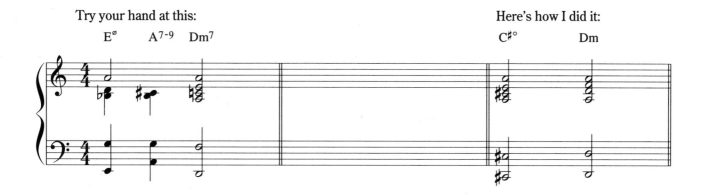

Here is how I used this in "My Melancholy Baby."

becomes

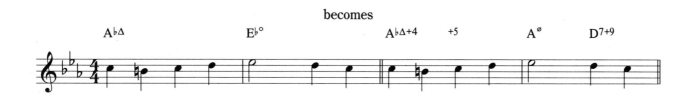

Harmonizing Melody Notes

9

Melody notes can be isolated from their existing harmonic underpinning and assigned new chords. There are three basic choices for harmonizing melody notes: 1) the melody note can become a chord member (or extension) of a new harmony. For example, if the melody note is F, and the original chord is D♭, we can change the chord to Cm11, thus making the melody note the eleventh (extension) of the new chord; 2) the melody note can be an *altered* chord tone. For example, if the melody note is G, and the original chord is C, we can change the chord to D♭7+11, thus making the melody note the +11 of the new (altered) chord; 3) the melody note can be a non-chordal tone. For example, if the melody note is F, and the original chord is Dm7, we can change the chord to Em7, thus making the melody note a non-chordal tone. Factors in choosing which setting is best for the melody note include the context of the substitution (what precedes and follows it), and the amount of consonance or dissonance desired.

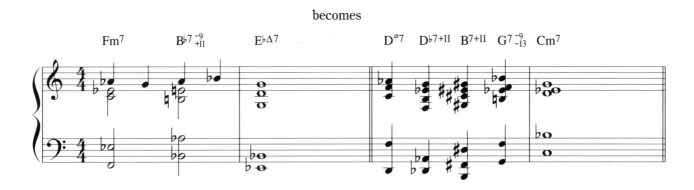

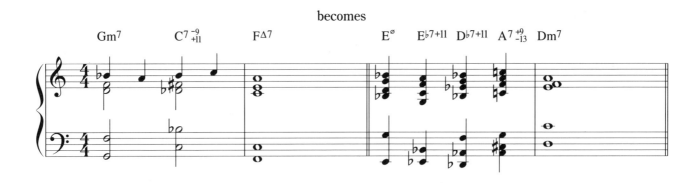

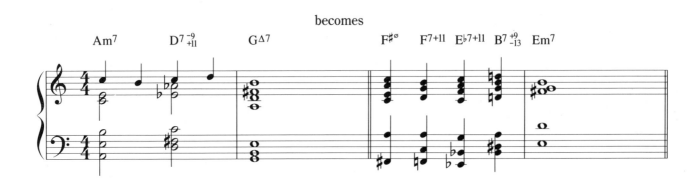

20

becomes

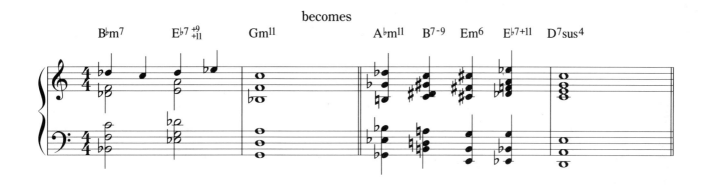

becomes

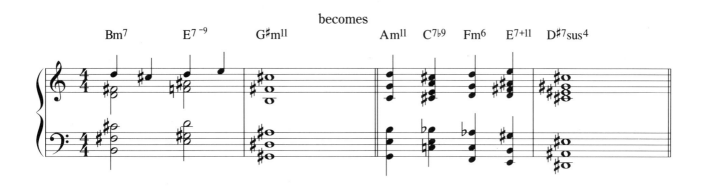

Try your hand at this:

Here's how I did it:

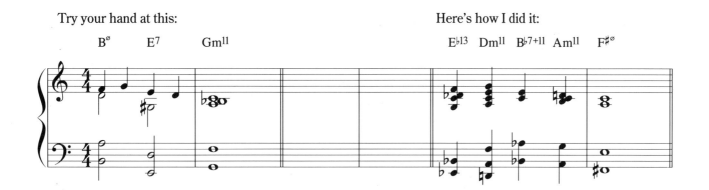

Here is how I used this device in "A Nightingale Sang In Berkeley Square."

becomes

Pedal Points

10

The movements of roots in the bass can be replaced with a common tone over which the harmonies move. This constant bass note can provide contrast to more active root movements. It can also imply alternative moods and colors to the harmonic content. This device is especially effective in the bridge sections of tunes. For example, we can take the common progression of III, VI7, II, V7, I (Em, A7, Dm, G7, C) and place a pedal point of G under the entire progression.

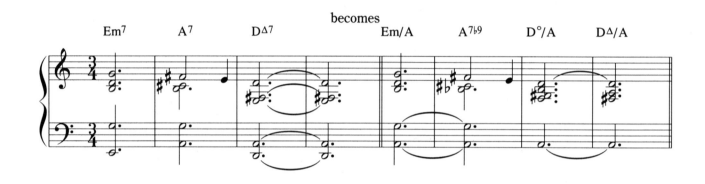

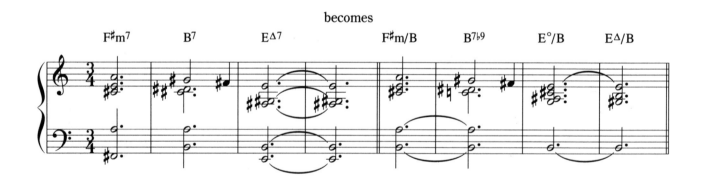

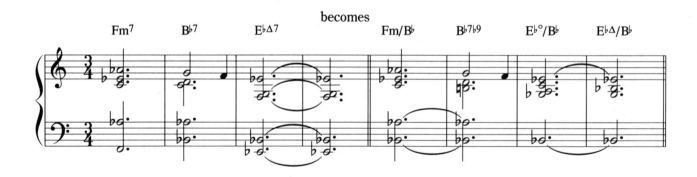

becomes

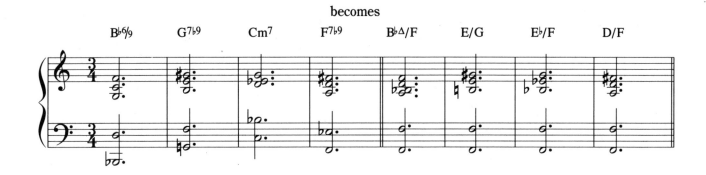

becomes

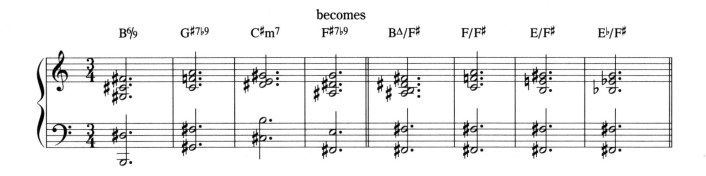

Try your hand at this:

Here's how I did it:

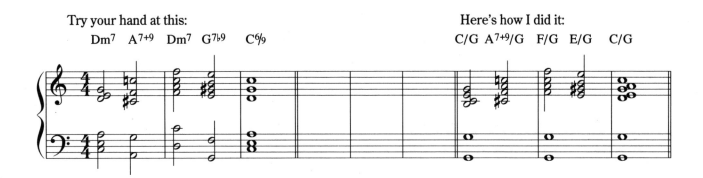

Here is how I used the device of pedal point in my arrangement of "A Nightingale Sang In Berkeley Square."

becomes

Use of Constant Structures

11 Constant structures can be used to harmonize a melody. Generally these are chords which move in parallel motion along with the melody. For example, if we have a melody line of C, B♭, A, we can build a structure underneath those melody notes based on the interval of a fourth. Going down from C, we can place the notes G, D, A, and E. This "quartal" structure can be moved in parallel motion under the prescribed melody notes. Therefore, the structure remains constant, with the melody.

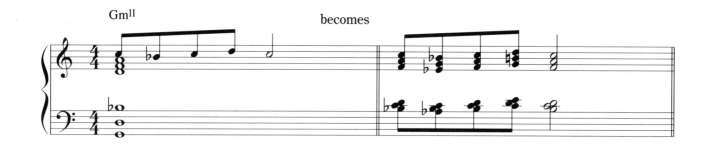

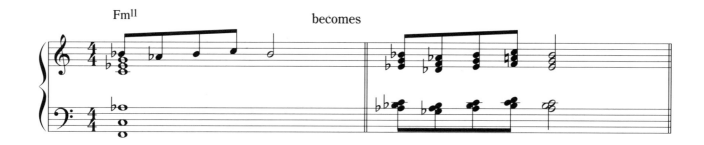

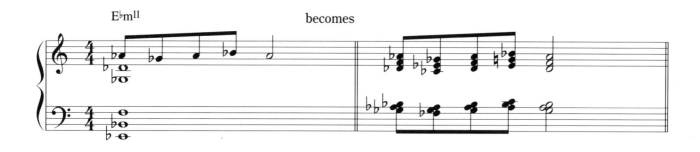

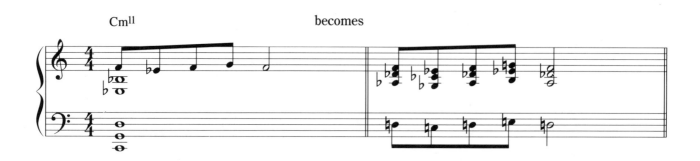

Am¹¹　　　　　　　becomes

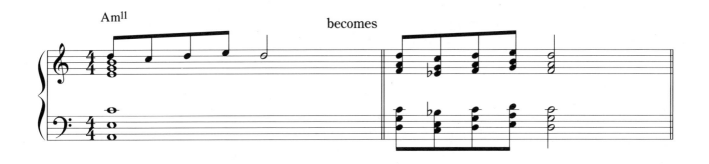

Try your hand at this:　　　　　　　Here's how I did it:

A⁷sus⁴

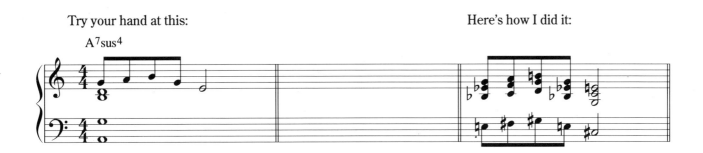

I used this device in my arrangement of "Darn That Dream."

becomes

Em　　G⁺　　D⁷　　C　　Dm¹¹　F♯m¹¹　A♭sus　G⁷sus　F⁷⁺¹¹　E♭⁷⁺¹¹

Modulation — Changing Keys

12

This can be an effective way of altering the mood of a piece. Sections of a tune can modulate from the original key to create contrast. For example, if a tune with a structure of ABA were in the key of F Major, we might modulate up a minor third to the key of A♭ Major for the B sections (bridge) of the tune. This modulation could be accomplished by approaching the "new" key with a ii, V7 progression in the new key. (B♭m, E♭7, A♭). Another alternative is to have the melody remain in the original key while the harmonies are placed in a new tonal center. This technique keeps the melodic line intact while changing the color of the tune's harmonic underpinning.

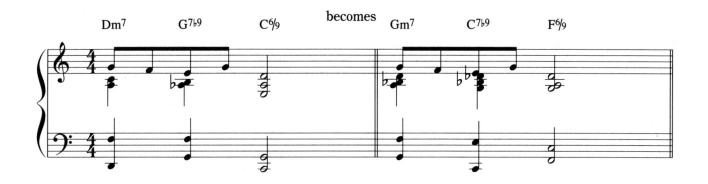

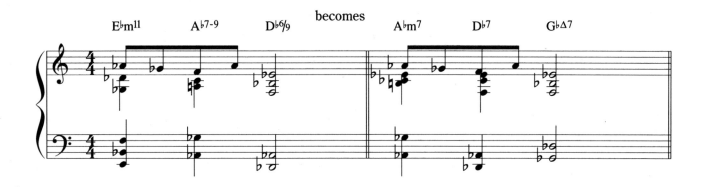

Try your hand at this:

Here's how I did it:

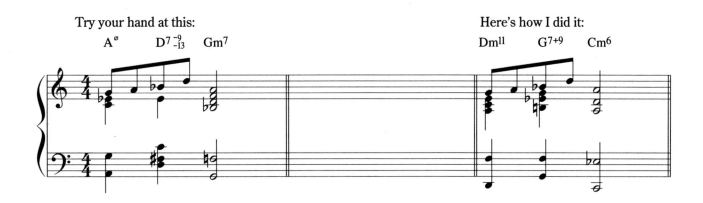

I used the device of keeping the melody intact but changing the harmonic progression under it in my arrangement of "Cherokee."

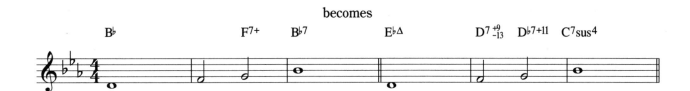

Contrary Motion

13

Contrary motion between the two outer voices (melody and bass) can yield new harmonies and provide new melodic interest. If we have a melody that ascends from C, chromatically (in half-steps) to E♭, we can place harmonies under it which have a bass movement of descending motion. This motion can either mirror the intervallic movement of the melody or use a different intervallic relationship to provide more contrast while still moving constantly in a descending line. This bass movement can consist of roots of chords, inversions of chords, or a combination. The same technique can be used if we have a melody which descends, resulting in an ascending bass line.

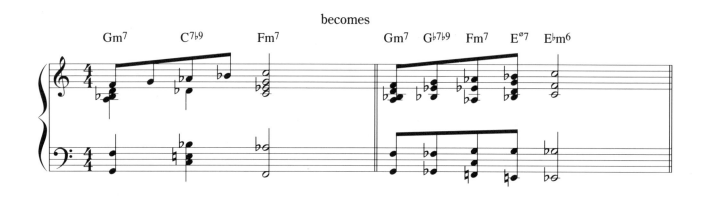

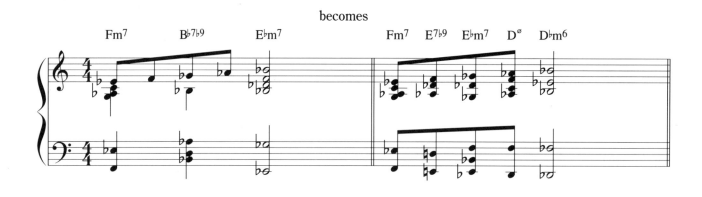

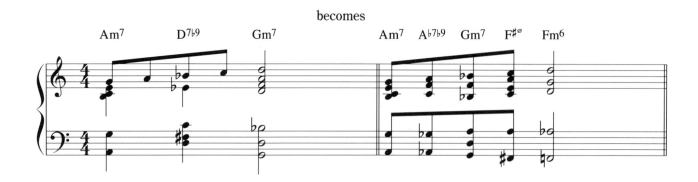

becomes

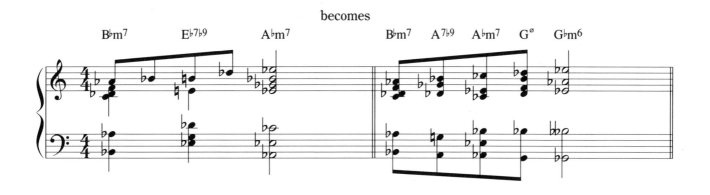

becomes

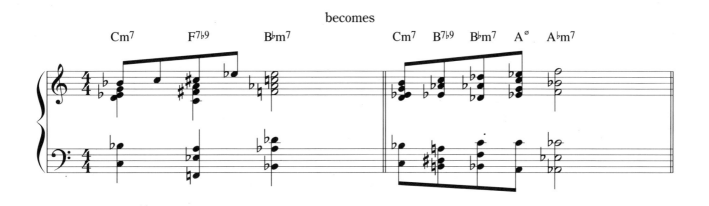

Try your hand at this: Here's how I did it:

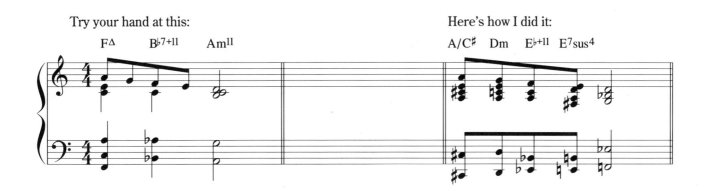

I used contrary motion in "My Melancholy Baby."

becomes

Descending Bass/Ascending Bass

14

The bass line can be treated independently of the melody, and can move in either a constant upward or downward motion. (Inverting chords can aid this process.) Once again, the intervals used in such movement can vary. Half-steps, whole steps, minor or major thirds, or larger intervals can be employed.

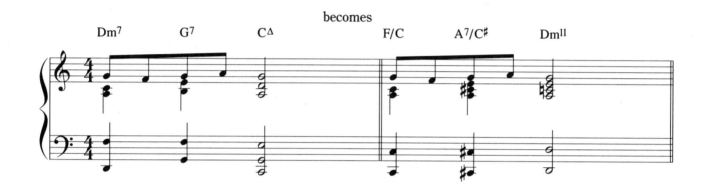

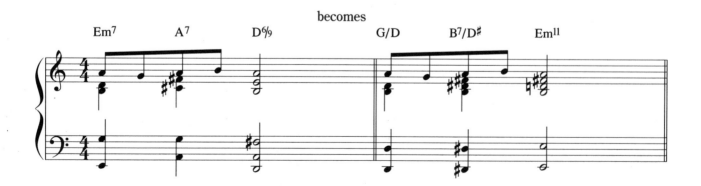

becomes

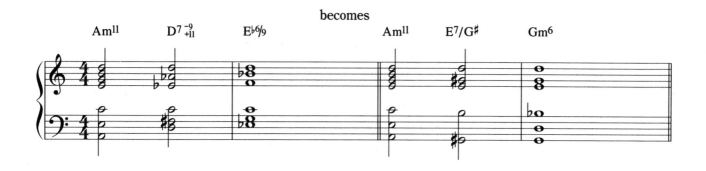

becomes

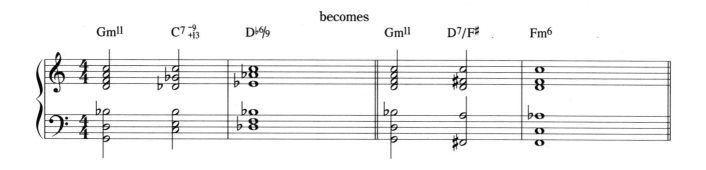

Try your hand at this:

Here's how I did it:

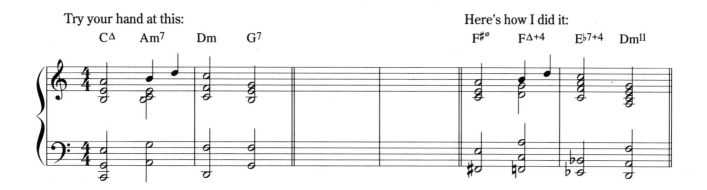

I used this technique in my arrangement of "Solitude."

becomes

Suspended Sounds

15

Chords which contain thirds can be suspended (the third is then replaced with a fourth) which creates an unusual harmonic color. These suspensions can permanently replace the third, or they can resolve to the third. The resolution will yield inner voice movement. If, for example, we had the progression Cm, F7, B♭, we could change the qualities of these chords by keeping the root movement the same while assigning the suspended quality to each chord. Thus the progression would become Dsus.4, G7sus.4, Csus.4. Generally, a sus.4 chord contains a dominant seventh. Since the third is usually missing, it is sometimes difficult to determine if a major or minor quality is indicated. The major 7 interval is less frequently used in a sus.4 chord, but it does appear occasionally (i.e. C Maj.7sus.4). This is a somewhat harsher sound given the dissonant quality of the major 7 interval.

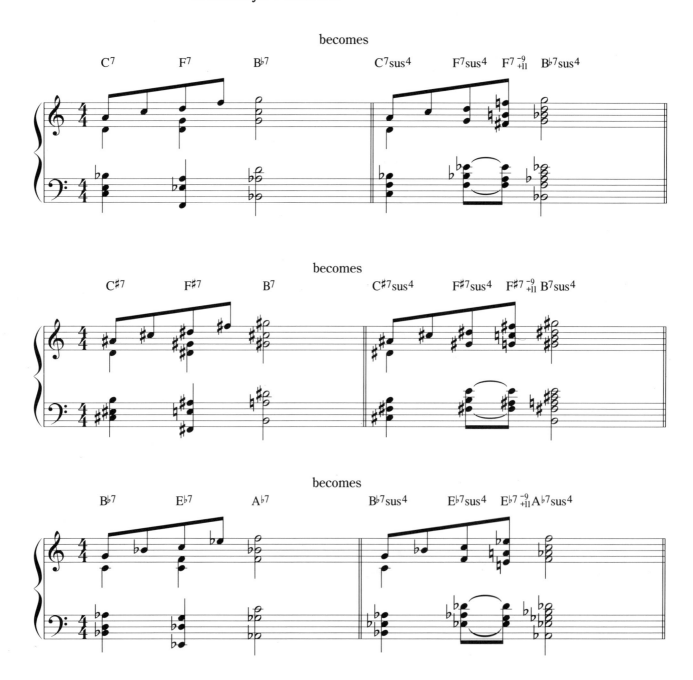

becomes

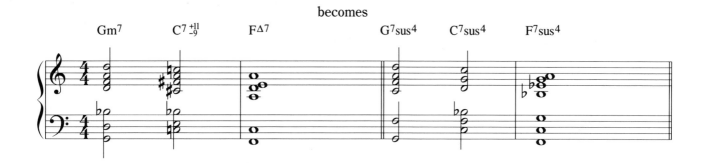

becomes

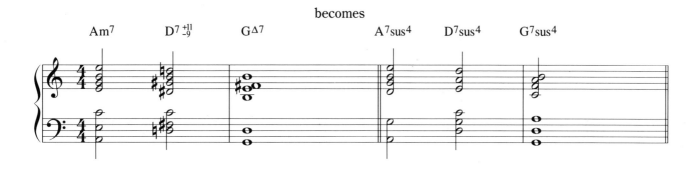

Try your hand at this:

Here's how I did it:

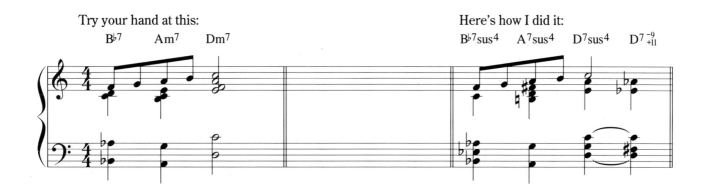

I used suspended sounds in my arrangement of "Indiana."

becomes

Inserting Additional Chords

16

Chords can be placed between existing chords to provide more harmonic movement and interest. Combining some of the previously mentioned techniques, such as tritone substitution, approach chords, descending/ascending bass lines, suspended chords, and arbitrary root movement while keeping existing harmonies can yield a dense harmonic palette. Since this category is a virtual composite of most of the previously mentioned techniques, the final results can best be demonstrated in the versions of each tune that follow.

Manipulation of Musical Forms

17

Rhythmic diminution (making rhythmic values shorter), rhythmic augmentation (making rhythmic values longer), adding measures to musical phrases, taking away beats or measures from phrases, adding contrasting sections to existing structures are all possibilities in creative arranging. None of these techniques were used in the standards portion of this book. The musical forms of these tunes were kept intact to fully demonstrate the techniques described above. However, the two original blues included in this collection use the techniques of manipulation of forms. "Blue Cycle" is a blues using the format of 12 bars, the most common found in blues. However, in the section set aside for melodic improvisation, the form has been extended by use of harmonic augmentation resulting in a structure which is 16 measures long. "Sabra" keeps the 12 bar structure, but adds another section (bridge) as a contrast. This bridge is actually a progression which is loosely based on the bridge of the tune "I Got Rhythm." In this instance, the use of tritone substitution disguises the more commonly known progression. So you see, any of these techniques can be used to enhance the harmonic quality of tunes which are familiar and they can lead you to actually creating your own compositions. Enjoy!

Special thanks to Bill Evans for helping me set and realize my harmonic goals.

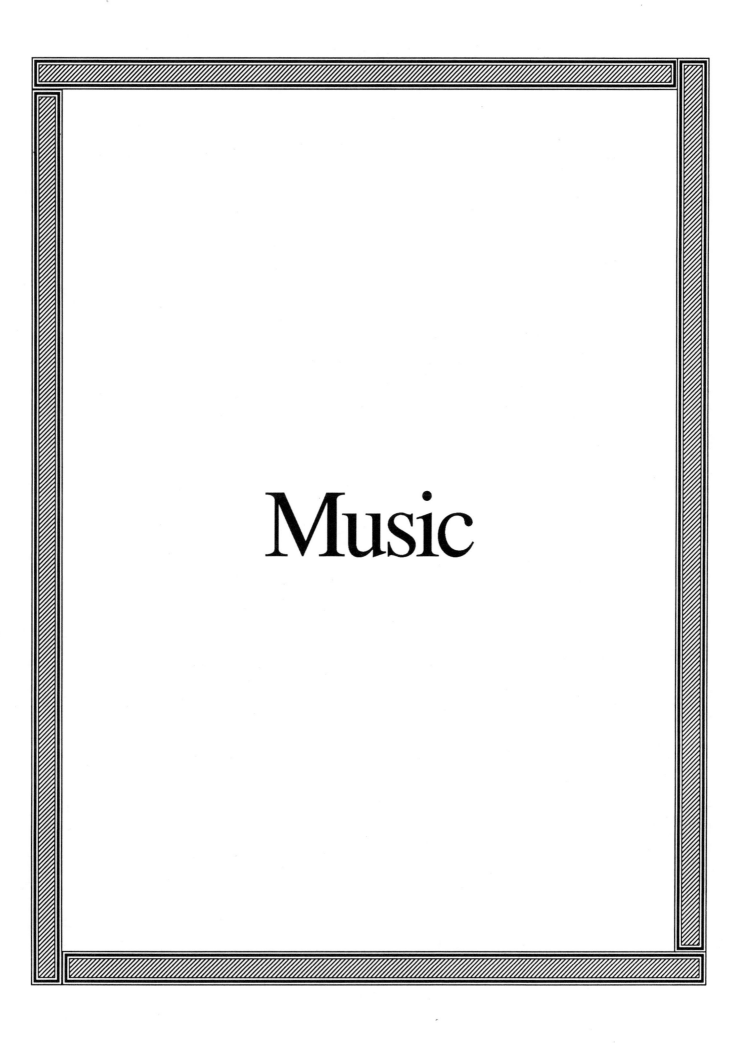

Music

CHEROKEE

Original Arrangement

By Ray Noble

CHEROKEE

Andy LaVerne Arrangement No.1

By Ray Noble

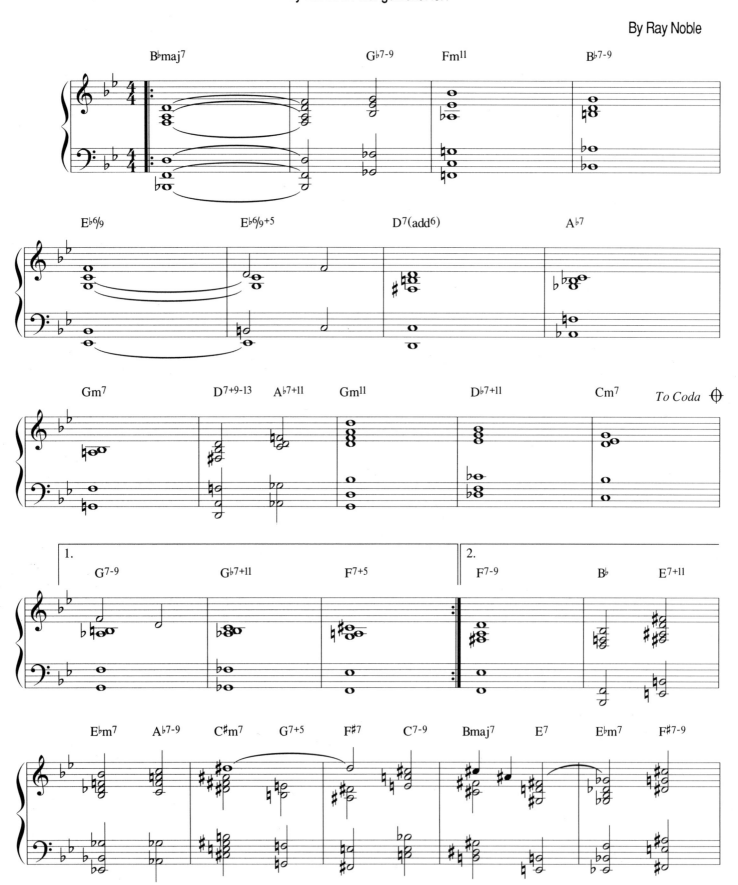

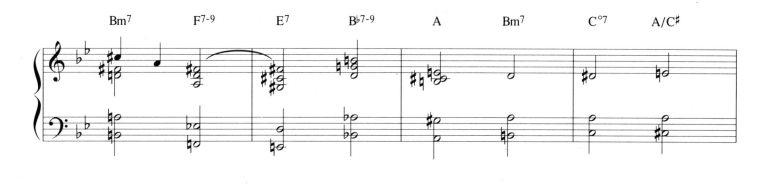

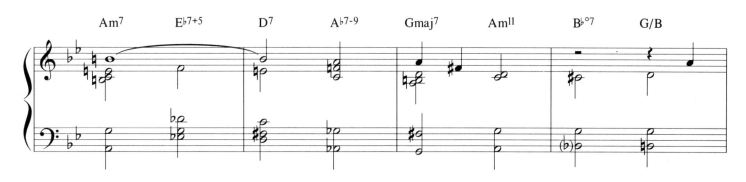

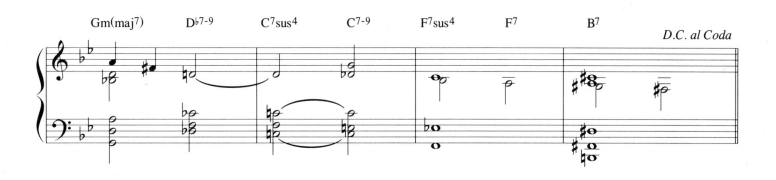

D.C. al Coda

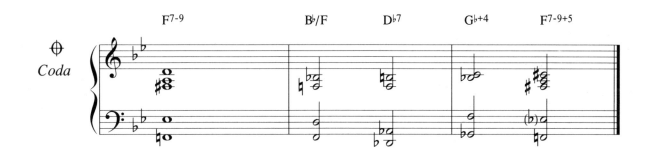

Coda

CHEROKEE

Andy LaVerne Arrangement No.2

By Ray Noble

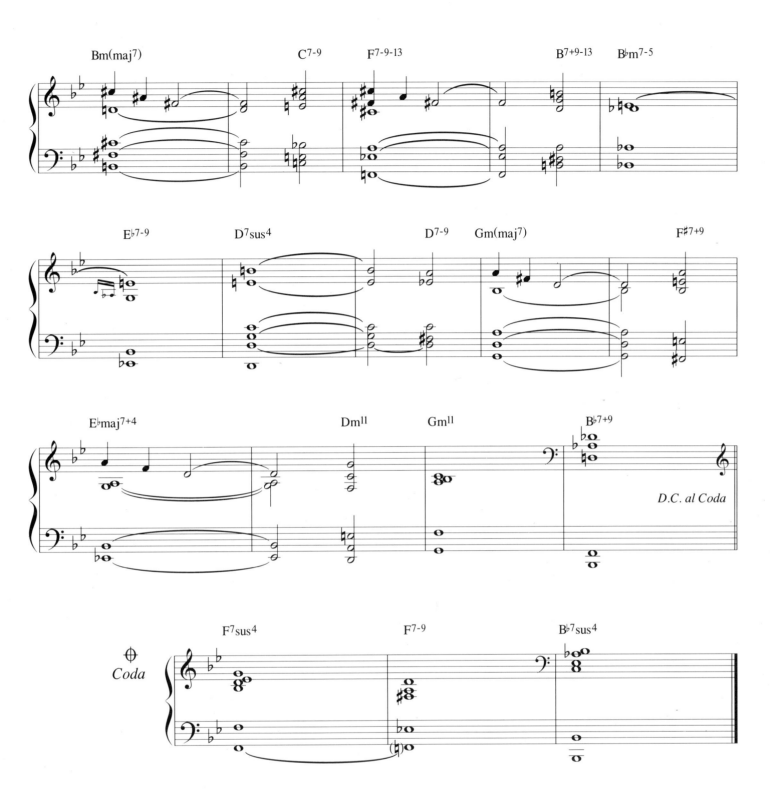

41

Darn That Dream

Original Arrangement

Lyric by Eddie DeLange
Music by Jimmy Van Heusen

Chorus Slowly (*Espress.*)

43

Darn your lips and darn your eyes, They lift me high a-bove the moon-lit skies, Then I tum-ble out of Par-a-dise, Oh Darn That Dream. Darn that one track mind of mine,___ It can't un-der-stand_ that you don't care_ Just to change the

Darn That Dream

Andy LaVerne Arrangement No.1

Lyric by Eddie DeLange
Music by Jimmy Van Heusen

Darn That Dream

Andy LaVerne Arrangement No.2

Lyric by Eddie DeLange
Music by Jimmy Van Heusen

EXACTLY LIKE YOU

Original Arrangement

Words by Dorothy Fields
Music by Jimmy McHugh

Exactly Like You

Andy LaVerne Arrangement No.1

Words by Dorothy Fields
Music by Jimmy McHugh

©1930 Aldi Music and Ireneadele Publishing Company pursuant to sections 304 (c) and 401 (b) of the U.S. Copyright Act. All rights administered by The Songwriters Guild of America

50

EXACTLY LIKE YOU

Andy LaVerne Arrangement No.2

Words by Dorothy Fields
Music by Jimmy McHugh

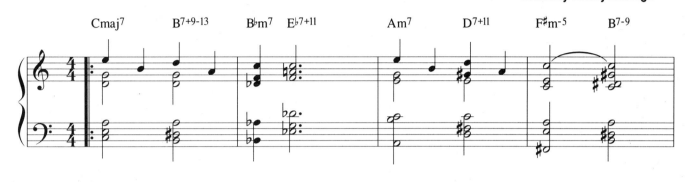

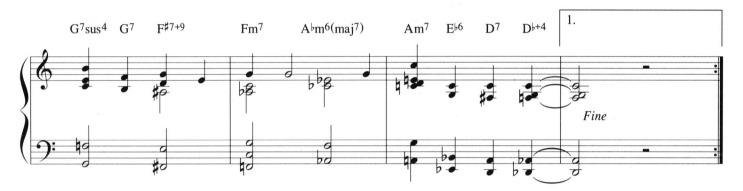

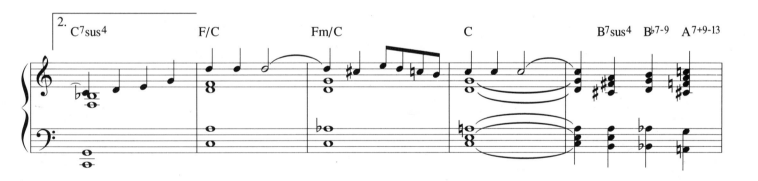

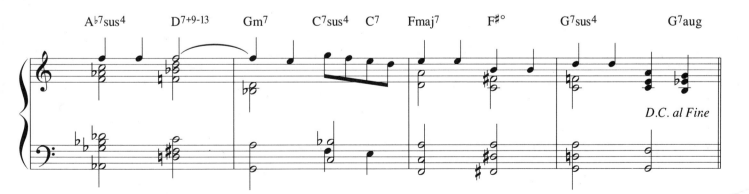

(Back Home Again In)
Indiana

Original Arrangement

Words by Ballard MacDonald
Music by James F. Hanley

CHORUS

Back home a-gain ____ In In-di-an-a, And it seems that I can see ____ The gleam-ing can-dle-light still shin-ing bright Thru the syc-a-mores for me, ____ The new mown hay ____ sends all its fra-grance From the fields I used to roam, ____ When I dream a-bout the moon-light on the Wa-bash, Then I long for my In-di-an-a home. Back home a- home. ____

(Back Home Again In)
Indiana
Andy LaVerne Arrangement No.1

Words by Ballard MacDonald
Music by James F. Hanley

(Back Home Again In)
Indiana

Andy LaVerne Arrangement No.2

Words by Ballard MacDonald
Music by James F. Hanley

Moonglow

Original Arrangement

By Will Hudson, Eddie DeLange
and Irving Mills

Moonglow

Andy LaVerne Arrangement No.1

By Will Hudson, Eddie DeLange
and Irving Mills

Moonglow

Andy LaVerne Arrangement No.2

By Will Hudson, Eddie DeLange
and Irving Mills

My Melancholy Baby

Original Arrangement

Words by George A. Norton
Music by Ernie Burnett

Slowly

VERSE

Come, sweetheart mine,   Don't sit and pine   Tell me of the cares that make you feel so blue
Birds in the trees,   Sweet mel-o-dies   They will take you to a land of peace-ful dreams

What have I done?   An-swer me, hon',   Have I ev-er said an un-kind word to you?
Clouds will roll by   Sha-dows will fly   Thru your open window while the pale moon beams

My love is true,   And just for you   I'd do al-most an-y-thing at an-y time
Why do you grieve   Try and be-lieve   Life is al-ways sunshine when the heart beats true

Dear, when you sigh   Or when you cry   Some-thing seems to grip this ve-ry heart of mine:
Ban-ish your fears   Smile through your tears   When you're sad   it makes me feel the same as you:

poco rall.

Guitar
CHORUS
Slowly(*with feeling*)

Come   to me, MY MEL - AN-CHO - LY   BA - BY   Cud-dle up and

don't   be   blue _____   All your fears are fool-ish fan - cy   may -

be   You know, dear, that I'm in love with you _____ Ev-'ry cloud must

have a sîl-ver li - ning   Wait un-til the sun shines through ___

_ Smile, my hon-ey dear While I kiss a-way each tear Or else I shall be.

poco rall.   *ten*   *rit molto*

mel - an - cho - ly, too. _____   too. ___

MY MELANCHOLY BABY

Andy LaVerne Arrangement No.1

Words by George A. Norton
Music by Ernie Burnett

MY MELANCHOLY BABY

Andy LaVerne Arrangement No.2

Words by George A. Norton
Music by Ernie Burnett

65

Picnic
(Theme From "Picnic")
Original Arrangement

Words by Steve Allen
Music by George W. Duning

PICNIC
(THEME FROM "PICNIC")

Andy LaVerne Arrangement No.1

Words by Steve Allen
Music by George W. Duning

PICNIC
(THEME FROM "PICNIC")

Andy LaVerne Arrangement No.2

Words by Steve Allen
Music by George W. Duning

Solitude
Original Arrangement

Words by Eddie DeLange and Irving Mills
Music by Duke Ellington

Solitude
Andy LaVerne Arrangement No.1

Words by Eddie DeLange and Irving Mills
Music by Duke Ellington

Solitude

Andy LaVerne Arrangement No.2

Words by Eddie DeLange and Irving Mills
Music by Duke Ellington

WRAP YOUR TROUBLES IN DREAMS
(AND DREAM YOUR TROUBLES AWAY)

Original Arrangement

Words by Ted Koehler and Billy Moll
Music by Harry Barris

WRAP YOUR TROUBLES IN DREAMS
(AND DREAM YOUR TROUBLES AWAY)

Andy LaVerne Arrangement No.1

Words by Ted Koehler and Billy Moll
Music by Harry Barris

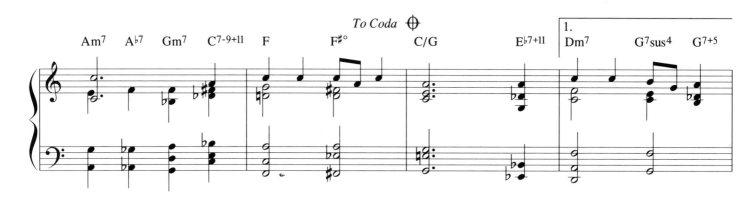

Wrap Your Troubles In Dreams
(And Dream Your Troubles Away)

Andy LaVerne Arrangement No.2

Words by Ted Koehler and Billy Moll
Music by Harry Barris

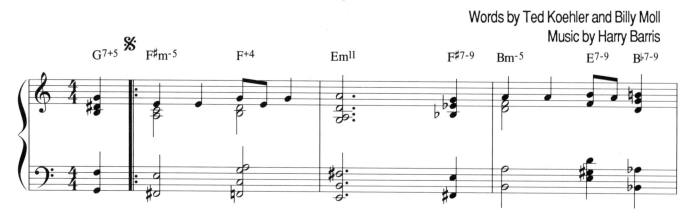

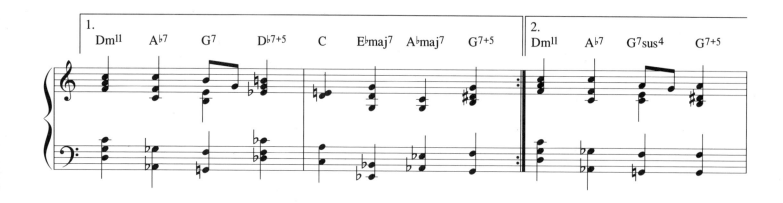

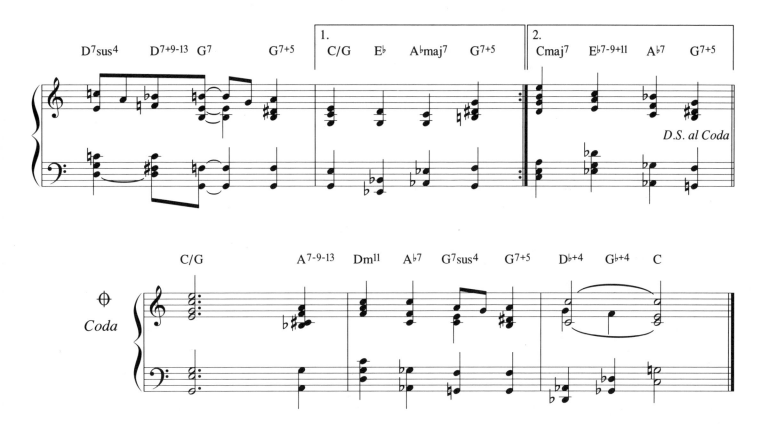

A Nightingale Sang In Berkeley Square

Original Arrangement

Lyric by Eric Maschwitz
Music by Manning Sherwin

know such en-chant-ment can be 'Cause it hap-pened one ev'-ning to me. ___

CHORUS

That cer - tain night, The night we met, There was
(How) strange it was, How sweet and strange, There was

ma - gic a-broad in the air There were an-gels din - ing at the Ritz, And A
ne - ver a dream to com-pare With that ha - zy, cra - zy night we met, When A

NIGHT - IN - GALE SANG IN BER - K'LEY SQUARE I
Pronounced (Bar - kley) This

81

SQUARE

82

whole darn world seemed up-side down The streets of town were paved with stars It was
that a dream or was it true?" Our home-ward step was just as light As the

such a ro-man-tic af-fair And as we kiss'd and said "good-night" A
tap-dan-cing feet of As-taire And like an e-cho far a-way A

NIGHT-IN-GALE SANG IN BER - K'LEY SQUARE _____
(Bar - kley)

How SQUARE

I know 'cause I was there That night in Ber-k'ley Square. _____
(Bar-kley)

rall.

A Nightingale Sang In Berkeley Square

Andy LaVerne Arrangement No.1

Lyric by Eric Maschwitz
Music by Manning Sherwin

A Nightingale Sang In Berkeley Square

Andy LaVerne Arrangement No.2

Lyric by Eric Maschwitz
Music by Manning Sherwin

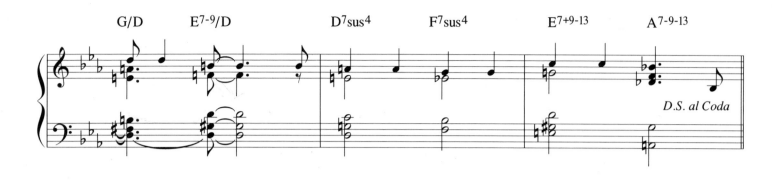

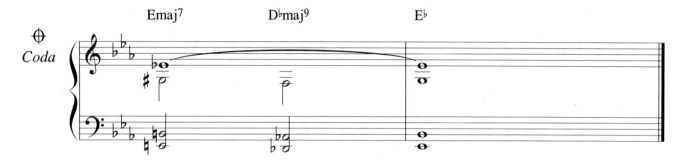

Sabra

By Andy LaVerne

BLUE CYCLE

By Andy LaVerne

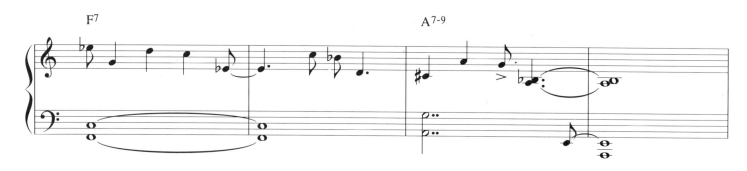

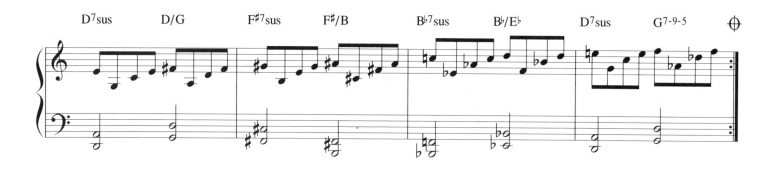

Chords for Solos:

𝄆 C^7	%	%	%
F^7	%	A^{7-9}	%
C/D	D/G	E/F♯	F♯/B
A♭/B♭	B♭/E♭	C/D	G^{7-9-5} 𝄇

Andy LaVerne

Born in New York City on December 4, 1947, Andy LaVerne enrolled at the age of 8 in the Juilliard School of Music as a classical piano student, and he continued the study of music at the New York City High School of Music and Art, Ithaca College, Berklee College of Music, and the New England Conservatory.

As a teenager, LaVerne discovered jazz by listening to "Monk's Dream" by Thelonious Monk on the radio. His interest for jazz piano eventually led him to Bill Evans, who became his first jazz teacher. Later on he also studied jazz with Don Friedman, Jackie Byard, and Richard Beirach. He continued his classical studies with John Ranck, and also studied composition with composer Karel Husa.

Andy LaVerne's professional career includes three years (1973-1975) with Woody Herman's big band and four years (1977-1980) as pianist, composer and arranger with the Stan Getz Quartet. He has also played and recorded with Frank Sinatra, Sonny Stitt, Donald Byrd, John Abercrombie, Miroslav Vitous, Lee Konitz, David Liebman, Joe Farrell, Eddie Harris, Scott Hamilton, Eddie Daniels, Dizzy Gillespie, Chick Corea, Bob Brookmeyer, Mel Lewis, Mel Torme, Bill Watrous, Shelly Manne, Eddie Gomez, and numerous other top performers.

His collaborations with Chick Corea resulted in the highly acclaimed album, "Andy LaVerne Plays The Music Of Chick Corea" (Jazzline). His growing list of recordings as leader includes "Another World," "For Us," "Frozen Music," "Fountainhead," "Severe Clear," "Standard Eyes" (SteepleChase), "Liquid Silver," "Jazz Piano Lineage," "Magic Fingers" (DMP), "Natural Living" (Musidisc), "True Colors" (Pony Canyon), "See How It Feels" (Brubeck/LaVerne Trio, Blackhawk), and "Captain Video" (Atlas). New for 1991 is an L.A. recording featuring bassist John Patitucci, drummer Dave Weckl (both of Chick Corea's band) and saxist Bob Sheppard, tentatively titled "The Pleasure Seekers" (Triloka).

Andy LaVerne is the recipient of three Jazz Fellowships from the National Endowment for the Arts (1984, 1987, 1989). He has also been awarded several ASCAP composer awards as well as a "Meet The Composer" grant.

His first instructional video, "Andy LaVerne's Guide to Modern Jazz Piano," has recently been released by Homespun Tapes. LaVerne has been the subject of feature articles in "Downbeat," "Keyboard," "Jazziz" and "Hot House."

When not touring North America and Europe playing concerts, clubs, and giving clinics, he is a frequent contributor to "Keyboard," "Downbeat," "Piano Stylist," "Keyboard Classics," "Sheet Music Magazine," "Letter From Evans," and other publications. He has also served as an adjunct professor of music at The University of Bridgeport.